The Teen Girl's Gotta-Have-It Guide™ to

boys

From Getting Them
to Getting *Over* Them!

By Jessica Blatt

Illustrated by Cynthia Frenette

Watson-Guptill Publications/New York

Senior Acquisitions Editor: Julie Mazur
Editor: Cathy Hennessy
Designer: Margo Mooney
Production Manager: Katherine Happ

Text copyright © 2007 by Jessica Blatt
Illustrations copyright © 2007 by Cynthia Frenette

First published in 2007 by Watson-Guptill Publications,
a division of VNU Business Media, Inc.
770 Broadway, New York, NY 10003
www.wgpub.com

ISBN-10: 0-8230-1725-7
ISBN-13: 978-0-8230-1725-6

Library of Congress Cataloging-in-Publication Data

Blatt, Jessica.
　The girl's gotta-have-it guide to boys : from getting them to getting
over them! / Jessica Blatt ; illustrated by Cynthia Frenette.
　　　p. cm.
　Includes index.
　ISBN-13: 978-0-8230-1725-6 (alk. paper)
　ISBN-10: 0-8230-1725-7 (alk. paper)
　1.　Teenage girls—Life skills guides—Juvenile literature. 2.　Teenage boys—
Psychology—Juvenile literature. 3.　Interpersonal relations in adolescence—
Juvenile literature. I. Frenette, Cynthia. II. Title.
　HQ798.B613 2007
　306.730835'2—dc22
　　　　　　　　　　　　　2006025079

Printed in China

First printing, 2007

1 2 3 4 5 6 7 8 9 / 15 14 13 12 11 10 09 08 07

To my parents, for living the ultimate love story *every day*— and still acting like two crazy-in-love teenagers. I love you!

And for Matt, my #1 crush. I love you, always.

nts

introduction

Ah, boys.

You love 'em. You hate 'em. Some days you can't get enough of them, and other days they're simply *too* much to handle!

But if there's one thing that's always true about guys, it's that they have a way of bringing up a *bazillion* new questions for you to think about—like how to know when the guy *you* like likes you back, or if it's okay to date a friend's crush, or whether you'll be ready when kissing comes knocking on your door!

That's where this book comes in: *The Teen Girl's Gotta-Have-It Guide to Boys* is your handy little tool box for dealing with guys— and the good and bad that comes with 'em.

Getting to Know . . . You

When everything's going great with guys, the world looks rosy. You love everyone around you and yourself, too!

But, sometimes, the most frustrating thing about guys is dealing with the days when things *don't* go well—on those days, it's like they set up shop in your brain and make you feel insecure or doubtful or just plain cranky. Which is why the most important thing you can do when it comes to guys is realize that *you are amazing with or without them*. A guy doesn't define you—your personality, sense of humor, talents, passions, and interests are what make you who you are! So even during the hardest times—like during a breakup or after a rejection—remember that *you* define your image and self-worth. Guys don't.

So before you get all caught up in—or start to feel all down about—guys, use the next page to make a list of all the things you love about yourself, and your goals that have absolutely *nothing* to do with guys. It may sound corny, but remember this: Guys can be icing on the cake, but even without them life is pretty sweet!

Things that Make Me **Happy**

My favorite thing to do in my free time is:

The talent I'm most proud of is:

I'm good at helping other people with:

I love my:

My secret funny talent is:

My favorite subject at school is:

The people I enjoy spending time with are:

One day I'd love to travel to:

Before I graduate from high school, I want to:

After high school, I hope to someday:

As you tear through the pages in this book, remember that you and your life are awesome—with or without a guy!

The Teen Girl's Gotta-Have-It RULES for Dealing with Boys AKA: S.T.R.O.N.G.

No matter who your crush is or what your relationship status is, here are six golden rules to keep in mind for dealing with boys.

go SLOWLY It can be easy to get swept up in the fun of meeting a new guy, but if you rush to spend all of your time with him or to speed up your relationship, there will be less to look forward to later. So treat a new guy like you would a new friend—you may click instantly, but it takes time to *truly* get close.

TRUST your gut It's great when you meet someone who teaches you new things and opens your eyes to ideas you've never thought about. But don't give up the things that matter most to *you*—listen to your instincts, and stay true to yourself.

be RESPECTFUL Whether you're trying to lure a guy in or trying to break up with him, there's nothing good that can ever come out of acting cruelly. You can stand your ground—and even play tough—but you'll only regret it later if you choose to be mean.

be OPEN The best thing about any relationship is when it teaches you something new—and teaches you something about yourself. It's easy to keep your mind open when things are going well; but even when things get tough or sour completely, focus on the fact that you'll learn about relationships in ways that will help you later.

NURTURE your friendships Guys may come and go, but real friends are forever—so don't forget to devote time to them, no matter *how* much you get caught up in a guy.

GIGGLE Things can get sticky and tricky with guys, but if you remind yourself not to take them too seriously all the time, you'll be happier all around and have more fun. Remember to laugh at yourself—and to do fun, silly activities with guys instead of only being way intense.

who do

you like?

Remember all those fairy tales you heard about Prince Charming? And those games you played with your Ken doll? And the movies you saw about the always-gorgeous captain of the football team?

Well, it's time to tune out *all* of those images, and understand the most important thing about guys: None of them—*not a single one of them out there*—is perfect.

And to make matters more confusing, there's no one "type" of guy that's better than other guys. In fact, the only lesson you can and should take away from all of those movies and love songs is that, sometimes, the guy you never thought of romantically *could* be the best one for you—and that the most important thing about any guy is how he makes you feel when you're with him.

Prince Charming Checklist

It can be hard to know who you like and who's right for you—especially if everyone in your school is caught up with liking the one guy who's the cutest or the most popular. But instead of just going after the guy—or the type of guy—whom everyone *else* likes, stop and think about the traits that are most important to *you*, and ask yourself the following about your crush:

1. Do you feel like you can be yourself around him?

2. Are you comfortable with him meeting your family and friends?

3. Do you have a lot to talk about?

4. Do you like the same things?

5. Do you have fun together?

6. Do you feel excited when you know you'll be seeing him?

7. Does he make you feel proud of yourself?

8. **Does he make you feel proud of him?**

9. **Do you trust him?**

10. **Do you miss him when he's gone?**

Dear Cutie,
Miss you!
Wish you were here!
XO Your B.F.

You probably already see where this exercise is going: If you answered "yes" to most of these questions, chances are you're already going after the kind of guy that's best for you. But if more of your answers are "sometimes" or "no," you might be chasing after (or spending time with) a guy who's all wrong for you!

But whether you're with your Mr. Right already or not sure if your crush is worth your time, remember this: No matter how a guy dresses or what music he listens to or what his family is like or where he comes from, there are five basic questions you should ask yourself about any crush or boyfriend:

1. **Do You Have Stuff in Common?** Sure, opposites attract— sometimes. And while it's important to have different interests from your crush and to teach each other new things, it's even more important to have certain really basic things in common—like your values, interests, and priorities. If you don't, your relationship can quickly become stressful, hard to balance, and not that much fun. So, no—you don't have to both be A students or varsity athletes or incredible musicians. But if you both respect the importance of say, outside interests and passions, you'll be more likely to support each other's goals (maybe he'll come to your soccer games, and you'll go to his jazz concerts), instead of resenting them. And not everyone has the best relationship with their parents or loves school— but if you have similar attitudes about the importance of things like family or good grades, you'll be more likely to understand each other and relate to each other's feelings.

2. Do You Feel Comfortable With Him? Everyone wants to make a good impression around their crush—and that's part of flirting (more on that in the next chapter!). But if you find yourself always trying to look or act perfectly—or differently—around your crush, there's a good chance you two just aren't meant to be. Think about it: If you're spending all of your energy trying to be "perfect," how much energy can you possibly have left to put into getting to know him, letting him get to know you, and doing fun things together? Sure, no one wants their crush to see them when they're at their lowest—especially in the beginning of a new relationship— but ask yourself how your crush would react if he saw you with a runny nose and in your comfiest PJs. If he'd melt over how cute you look, you might have a keeper. But if it would send either of you running, maybe he's not boyfriend material after all . . .

3. Does He Respect You—And Do You Respect Him? Having things in common often leads to mutual respect. But even if you have everything in the *world* in common, ask yourself if he treats you the way you want to be treated. Does he introduce you to his friends— or does he act like he doesn't know you when they're around? Does he flirt with other girls in front of you—or does he make you the center of attention? Does he give you girl-time or work-time or family-time when you want it—or does he get angry if you're not free when he wants to hang out? A good guy doesn't have to kiss the ground you walk on or put you on a pedestal (which doesn't sound like much fun for either of you!)—but he *should* treat you with the same level of respect your closest friends do.

4. Do You Trust Him? Pure honesty and trust don't come overnight in any relationship—think how long it may have taken you to tell even your best friend your closest secrets! But if you've ever caught him in a lie or if he's cheated on you or pressured you into doing something, he simply might not be mature enough for you—or have the same values and attitudes that you do.

5. Does He Excite You? While numbers 1–4 are super-important, you can't play down how key attraction really is in a relationship. So you could have comfort, things in common, respect, and trust— but if you're not dying to kiss him or hug him or squeeze him every time you see him, he may not be right for you. Attraction isn't always rational—you can't make yourself feel a spark with even the greatest guy in the world, and you may find yourself attracted to someone everyone else seems to overlook.

A FINAL NOTE

Attraction can't *always* be explained—that's part of the fun and the mystery and the excitement of relationships! And while there's no exact formula for figuring out how your mysterious heart works, remember this:

> The most important thing in any relationship
> is how it makes you feel while you're in it.
> Look for boys you connect with in ways
> that matter to you—and who make you feel as
> special as you are!

flirting

101

Flirting is an art.

Sure, some people seem like they were *born* good at it—you probably know at least one girl who's been perfectly comfortable flirting ever since you were in elementary school. But flirting is also the kind of thing that you can learn and, with some practice, master. And, at the end of the day, flirting isn't complicated when you see it for what it really is: a fun way to connect with people, make a positive impression, and leave them intrigued and wanting to know more about you.

You can casually flirt with anyone—but you don't want to mislead or tease guys, either. And the secret to balancing both comes down to two things: Knowing what you want (Do you want him to ask you to an upcoming dance? To kiss you? To be your boyfriend? Or just to notice you?)—and finding a way that's comfortable for you to get it.

If you know what you want, you'll feel confident about dropping some of your shyness and focusing on your goal, *and* you'll be less likely to just lead a guy on or tease him for no reason.

So turn the page, and let's get flirtin'!

What Kind of Flirt Are You?

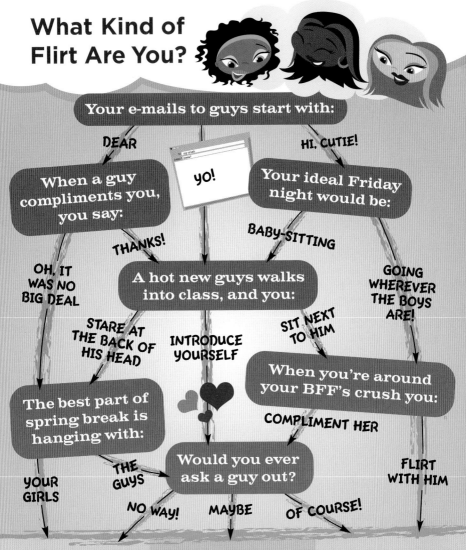

Your e-mails to guys start with:

DEAR → When a guy compliments you, you say:

yo!

HI, CUTIE! → Your ideal Friday night would be:

THANKS! → A hot new guys walks into class, and you:

OH, IT WAS NO BIG DEAL

BABY-SITTING

GOING WHEREVER THE BOYS ARE!

STARE AT THE BACK OF HIS HEAD

INTRODUCE YOURSELF

SIT NEXT TO HIM → When you're around your BFF's crush you:

The best part of spring break is hanging with:

COMPLIMENT HER

Would you ever ask a guy out?

YOUR GIRLS

THE GUYS

FLIRT WITH HIM

NO WAY!   MAYBE   OF COURSE!

BASHFUL BABE Modesty and politeness are great traits—but they can keep you from getting what you really want. So the next time you're around your crush, take a small risk, like saying "Hi."

CONFIDENT CAT You're confident and outgoing—without being overbearing—and your natural friendliness will attract guys to you. When you do start dating, remember to stay true to the kind of person and friend you are.

FICKLE FLIRT Guys don't scare you! But, sometimes, your guts may drive guys away. Be selective with the guys you shower with attention. If you flirt with everyone, you'll end up making one guy feel no more special than the next.

The Flirting Fundamentals

Now that you know where you stand—and the ways you could stand to do more, or less—let's get down to business with the dos and don'ts of flirting.

Make like Oprah.

DO ask him questions about himself and really listen to his answers. This will do three things: First, it will help you get to know more about him. Second, it will lessen any self-consciousness you may be feeling, because you'll be shifting the spotlight off of you and on to him. And, third, it will give you a foundation of things to talk about the *next* time you see him.

DON'T bombard him with nonstop questions or ask deeply personal questions—you want him to see that you're considerate and interested, not nosy! So stick to common ground, like his interests and his friends and school.

fast fix

If you find yourself near your crush with absolutely *nothing* to say, ask him a question you secretly know he'll have the answer to—like where the nurse's office is, or if your spring break starts on a Friday or a Monday.

Take mental notes.

DO pay attention to things about him that other people might not notice—like a thoughtful answer he gives in class, or a band sticker he has on his notebook.

DON'T be a stalker or bring up things you found out about him through third parties. (Wouldn't *you* be creeped out if someone you didn't know well knew personal things about you?)

Speak your mind.

DO express your opinion—even if it's different from his. Any guy who's not intrigued by a girl with her own thoughts isn't worth your time anyway!

DON'T be closed-minded about opinions of his that are different from yours. There are two sides to every argument!

Have a supporting cast.

DO keep your friends around, to talk you up in front of your crush and so that he can meet the people who are important to you.

DON'T *always* surround yourself with a gaggle of friends— or with friends who will flirt with your crush, instead of letting *you* have the spotlight!

Do *your* thing.

DO continue your hobbies and interests, even if it means having less time with him. Having talents and hobbies makes you interesting, and not being available 24/7 makes you intriguing! Plus, your interests will give you things to talk about and teach him.

DON'T take up hobbies *just* because your crush is into them—make sure *you're* interested in them, too. (Otherwise, if your crush fades, you could find yourself committed to a club, sport, or class you hate.)

Beware of your cell phone (and the computer).

DO use your gadgets to your advantage—like to send a funny joke, or text him a flirty message.

DON'T *only* talk to him via texting or e-mail. If you're ever going to be more than flirt-buddies, you'll have to make sure you can talk in *person*, too.

Open up.

DO let him get a sense of who you are by talking about your interests and letting your sense of humor—and kindness— shine through.

DON'T spill your entire life story during the "getting-to-know-you" phase; wait until you're both more comfortable with and trusting of each other.

Make the first move.

DO go after what you want—you don't have to sit around waiting for a guy to call you or ask you out!

DON'T beg him for attention or throw yourself at him. (Think about it: Don't *you* want the things that are at least a little bit harder to get?)

Give yourself props—literally.

DO wear or have something conversation-worthy on or with you—like a piece of gum you can offer him, or a shirt with a funny saying he can't help but talk to you about.

DON'T compromise who you are to get attention. You don't have to make risqué jokes or wear crazy outfits if that's not your style.

Make contact.

DO look him in the eye when you talk to him. It'll convey confidence—which is always magnetic—and will draw him to you. And if you're feeling comfortable, look for subtle ways to touch his arm, back, or shoulder while talking to him.

DON'T constantly touch him or stare at him with nothing to say. That will only confuse him at best, or freak him out at worst.

A FINAL NOTE

When it comes to flirting, your goal should be to have fun and to feel *excited* about your interactions—and to make him think about you when you're not around. So remember this:

Show and tell him *just* enough about you to make him want to know more. Flirting is about getting to know the surface— relationships are about going deeper.

decoding

guy-speak

Boys may speak the same language, but the things they say can leave you totally confused.

So instead of spending hours and hours analyzing every word with your girlfriends, take a few minutes to learn how to decode guy-speak. Then you can figure out what guys are saying, and know how to get through to them every time, too.

Guy Glossary

Guys may speak the same words as you—but they can mean them *totally* differently. Here's a quick guide to what means what in the world of guy-speak.

When a guy says: "I'll call you."

WHAT HE PROBABLY MEANS IS: "I'll call you—when I get around to it and if I don't forget or get caught up playing PlayStation or doing homework or going to practice or watching TV..."

THE BEST THING FOR YOU TO DO IS: Not wait around. It will be hard to keep from checking your voice mail and text messages every two seconds, but don't plan your day around the hope that a guy will call. Get out there and make the plans you were going to make; and if he *does* call, you can make plans for a day that works better for *you*.

When a guy says: "Wanna hang out some time?"

WHAT HE PROBABLY MEANS IS: "I think I want to get to know you better, but I'm still not 100 percent sure about *what* I want—that's why I'm being so vague—well, that and I'm afraid you'll reject me."

THE BEST THING FOR YOU TO DO IS: If you like him, suggest a day and activity that you feel comfortable with and will help him get to know you better—like taking him to your favorite pizza place, or going hiking. If you're not that into him anyway, let him do some pursuing to convince you why you should devote some time to him.

When a guy says: "I just want to be friends."

WHAT HE PROBABLY MEANS IS: "I don't want to be boyfriend/ girlfriend—and we may *not* end up being friends after this either."

THE BEST THING FOR YOU TO DO IS: Give yourself some time away from him. You may think you should go out of your way to keep a crush in your life, but since he's telling you that you're not his main priority, throw yourself into *your* other priorities instead of waiting to see if he'll change his mind.

When a guy says: "Hey!"

WHAT HE PROBABLY MEANS IS: "Hey!"

THE BEST THING FOR YOU TO DO IS: Say "Hey!" back—with a smile. It could lead to nothing or something—but you'll never know until you give him a chance to say more next time.

When a guy says: "Your friend is cute."

WHAT HE PROBABLY MEANS IS: "By talking to you about someone you're close to, I'm saying that I don't see *you* as girlfriend material."

THE BEST THING FOR YOU TO DO IS: Back off. If he really likes your friend, it's never worth starting drama with a friend over a guy. Even if she doesn't like him, you shouldn't have to convince a guy why you're great—and even if you did, you'd still always wonder if he was secretly thinking about your best friend.

When a guy says: "Lindsay Lohan/Hilary Duff/Paris Hilton is so hot."

WHAT HE PROBABLY MEANS IS: "I'm flirting with you by letting you know that I think about girls!"

THE BEST THING FOR YOU TO DO IS: Flirt back—tell him what famous *guys* you think are hot!

All guys are different and these are just *general* rules about the things they say and do. That said, the best way to figure out what a guy (or anyone, really) means is by trusting their *actions*—how they treat you when they're around—more than anything they say or e-mail or write. Because while trying to figure out what guys are saying can make you wish for a translator, action is *always* a more trustworthy language!

fast fix

Remember, humor is a good thing! Don't take yourself too seriously around your crush, and don't be afraid to tease him with your quick wit, either!

The Online Scene

Talking on the phone and face-to-face is only half the battle—you probably spend a whopping chunk of time "talking" to guys through e-mail and texting, too. And even though computers are supposed to make things *easier* for everyone, sometimes they have a funny way of making relationships more complicated. To help you deal, here's how to make your e-mails, texts, and IMs talk for *you*!

KEEP THINGS SHORT.

E-mail is best for making plans, letting someone know you're thinking of them, or flirting when you can't be face-to-face. But it's not the right way to pour your heart out, start a fight, or apologize—nothing beats face-to-face contact for serious matters of the heart.

TO my crush
SUBJECT pizza?

hi! would u like to go 4 pizza tomorrow nite?
call me!
ttyl!
:)
Me

DON'T WRITE ANYTHING YOU WOULDN'T WANT YOUR GRANDMA TO READ. You may feel more comfortable at the keyboard than you do in person, but the biggest risk with online "talking" is that anything you say can be printed out, forwarded, or posted to any website or blog. So as tempting as it may be, don't use your e-mail for anything so private that you'd cringe if it became public.

BEWARE OF THE BCC. BCC-ing someone else on your e-mails to a guy may seem like a good idea, but it could come back to haunt you. And if your crush finds out that you've been secretly revealing personal stuff to someone else, he may start to wonder what *else* you talk about behind his back—and in turn he may trust you less with his secrets. Plus, it's just plain mean: Think about how you would feel if a friend called you on the phone and didn't tell you that *another* friend was listening in on the line!

AVOID FORWARDING. Any time you forward a message from your crush to someone else, you take the chance that you'll accidentally hit "reply"—and that he'll see any comments you made about him. So if his e-mail—or your reaction to it—is in *any* way private, keep it between you and him. If you absolutely *have* to dissect every last word of it with your best friend, call and *read* it to her.

fast fix

If you find yourself stumped for the perfect e-mail reply, don't rush to respond. Instead, reply with a winking emoticon, like a ;) or a vague response like "LOL . . . TTYL!"

DON'T SEND RISQUÉ PICTURES. Digital cameras and phone cameras make it easy to quickly send along pics from parties and fun nights out. But just like you should never write something you wouldn't want the whole world to read, you shouldn't send him any private pictures, either!

A FINAL NOTE

As if reading guys' minds isn't hard enough, figuring out what guys mean can be just as frustrating. So here's something to keep in mind:

If you "listen" to guys' actions, you'll get by without a translator or a headache!

the deal

Once you've become a pro at flirting, you'll probably have all kinds of guys giving you attention!

But how can you tell if the guy *you* like likes you more than a friend—and if you two are headed toward "dating" or "being boyfriend and girlfriend" or "hanging out" or *whatever* your school may call it?

It can make you crazy just wondering if he sees you the same way you see him. But there *are* some tricks for figuring out your status!

Where Do You Stand?

Is a romance blooming, or is it just wishful thinking? Time to find out what your deal is! Write in your answers below—be honest!— then read on to figure out what's really going on.

YES or NO?

1.	Do the two of you talk in school?	
2.	Do you talk *outside* of school?	
3.	Do you e-mail?	
4.	Do you text?	
5.	Do you hang out outside of school with other people?	
6.	Do just the two of you hang out outside of school?	
7.	Have you ever been each other's date for a school event?	
8.	Did he remember your birthday?	
9.	Do you call each other for no particular reason?	
10.	Have you ever smooched?	

SCORING

If you answered yes to 3 or less: Right now, your crush is still just a crush, and it doesn't seem like you've made any *real* connection yet. Go to the chapter "Flirting 101" and try some of the tips to build up a gradual connection.

If you're short on time—because you're on vacation or at camp or in a situation where you have a limited chance to get to know him— cut to the chase and just approach him and say, "I know this may sound crazy, but since the summer/this vacation/*whatever* is running out, I didn't want to wait any longer to say that I was wondering if you'd want to hang out, before it's too late?" If he looks at you like you're crazy, don't panic—just say, "Okay, *that* didn't go as planned . . . but I'm glad I at least asked!" If he seems skeptical but willing to give it a try, have a specific activity or idea in mind (or see the chapter "Hanging Out" for some ideas). But remember: Jumping right from being strangers into hanging out comes with risks—like finding out he has a girlfriend, or having him tell other people you're into him. But if you don't have anything to lose and if you aren't putting yourself in any kind of danger, it can be worth daring yourself to take a chance!

(continued on the next page)

If you answered yes to 4 or 5: You two seem to be really connecting— but it looks like you haven't had enough opportunities to hang out outside of school, or alone together. So instead of waiting for him to ask *you* for plans, take some action and ask him to spend some time with you! If you feel weird asking him to hang out one-on-one, invite him and some of his friends to hang out with you and your friends or do something active and fun—go bowling or biking or swimming—where you'll have the chance to talk.

And if you *are* ready to hang out alone, here's how you should suggest it: Wait 'til a time when it's just the two of you at school— maybe when you're both at your lockers, or the last ones to leave class. Then, very casually suggest something specific to do. Pick something you're either a pro at and will feel confident doing with him (like going to the batting cages, or Rollerblading), or suggest something totally quirky that you've always *wanted* to do and think he'd enjoy, too—like playing paintball or taking a golf lesson.

If you answered yes to 6 or more: You two can't get enough of each other! The only thing that's missing from your relationship is the title boyfriend/girlfriend. And if that's what you're after, it's time to have "The Talk" (see next page).

Having "The Talk"

Dear Diary,
I REALLY like
Eric. I think
it's time for
THE TALK!

Talking with guys about relationships doesn't *have* to be awkward. The trick is to pick the right time and place—so that you'll feel comfortable asking for what you want, and he'll feel comfortable being honest with you about it. Here are some suggestions for making sure it all goes down smoothly.

THE SCENE: Pick a place where you're doing something active— like hanging out at the beach or at the mall, so that all of the attention isn't on your conversation.

THE CAST OF CHARACTERS: Just the two of you. You don't want his friends or your friends coming in and ruining the moment.

THE TIME: On a weekend or when neither of you are stressed about school, homework, classes, or family stuff.

THE SCRIPT (PICK A LINE THAT FEELS LIKE SOMETHING YOU'D SAY): "Hey, so I don't mean to sound all corny, but I just wanted to say that I have so much fun with you and was wondering what you thought of the whole being boyfriend/girlfriend thing . . . would you ever want to give that a try? **OR**

"Hey, I know this isn't the olden days when our parents 'went steady,' but what do you think of being boyfriend/girlfriend?" **OR**

"So . . . people have been asking me if we're boyfriend and girlfriend. I say no—but the truth is, I kinda wish we were. Do you?"

HIS PART: (Okay, so you won't know this part of the "script" until you give him a chance to react. Take a deep breath, and hear him out. If he's into it—yay! If he tells you that he's not into that kind of thing, respect that . . . and ask *him* to respect you by not repeating your conversation to other people. Either way, you'll have made what you want clear—which means that no matter *what* he says, you'll know you've put yourself out there, and you won't have regrets later.)

Dealing with a Bumpy Beginning

Once you two agree on what your "status" is, that doesn't mean everything will always be happy-smiley. Because having a "title" comes with its own share of obstacles— sometimes, you may feel like you don't know how to "act" now that you have a boyfriend. Here are some pointers.

If you feel like . . .

You don't always want to have to hang out or "check in" with him, but you don't want to insult or offend him, either . . .

TRY. . . Explaining to him that you love spending time with him, but that sometimes you like doing things on your own or with your girlfriends. Tell him that you know a relationship shouldn't just be on your terms—which is why you want him to feel comfortable telling you when *he'd* rather be alone or with the guys.

If you feel like . . .

Having a boyfriend means you can no longer hang out with your guy friends . . .

TRY . . . Hanging out with your new boyfriend *and* your guy friend— as long as you're sure your guy friend doesn't have an obvious crush on you! If he does, well, it's only fair for your boyfriend to feel uncomfortable about you two hanging out. As much as it may hurt you or your guy friend, you may have to pull back for a little while from hanging out or confiding in him as much. It may seem unfair, but think about it: How would *you* feel about your new boyfriend spending time with a girl who had a crush on him?

If you feel like . . .

Now that you have a boyfriend, you can't flop around in sweats— you always have to look hot for him . . .

TRY . . . Wearing what makes you feel comfortable and confident. If wearing sweats makes you feel your best, smartest, funniest, and most natural, then go on and wear 'em and if he doesn't love you in them, that's his problem. If dressing up makes you feel strong and confident and great, then feel free to dress up more than usual! What you wear doesn't and will never define who you are—but if the excitement of a new guy inspires you to have more fun with fashion, go for it. Just remember that you shouldn't have to change your whole look to impress or keep a guy.

A FINAL NOTE

We live in a world that's full of labels—so it's understandable that you might want one to define exactly what you and your crush are!

So when the timing and place and mood
are right, end the suspense and simply ask
for what you want.

hanging

out

Doesn't it feel like you wait all week for the weekend and then, when it comes, there's nothing good or new or fun to do?

And in terms of guys, it can feel like the only way to hang out is to go to a movie or to the mall or to one of your houses and watch TV! It can make you think there's something wrong with you that all you do is sit around without even having that much to say—snore!

The truth is that there are tons of fun and different things to do, no matter what your interests are or how tight of a couple you may be. And when you start doing fun and new things together, you'll grow closer because you'll share new experiences and create memories and inside jokes together.

The Guide to Great Dates

Believe it or not, there are fun things to do in *every* town, no matter where you live or how well you think you know your neighborhood. The secret is to pretend that your town is an exotic place you're visiting for the very first time, and to research it as if it's totally new. (Even grabbing something to eat can be exotic if you think outside the box!) So let the suggestions on the next few pages guide you to your best dates ever!

After School Dates

It can be tough to make time for each other after school—especially if you're both busy with homework and clubs and sports. The trick to great after-school dates is to choose activities that are relaxing, and don't go on for too long. That way, you can both unwind—but you'll still have time to take care of your responsibilities.

FREEBIE ACTIVITY
Make a difference:
Call the closest nursing home, soup kitchen, day care center, animal shelter, or children's hospital and ask how you two can help out for a few hours. Volunteering may not be the *first* thing you think of when you hear the word romance, but finding a cause you both believe in and working together can bring you closer. So spend an afternoon playing with

puppies at a local animal shelter, reading to the elderly at a local nursing home, or keeping kids company at a nearby day care center or children's hospital. It will make someone's day to have you around—and two hearts are always better than one.

OUTDOORSY ACTIVITY

Clean up: On a warm afternoon, ask a parent if you can wash his or her car. Then, get soap, a water supply (like the hose from your house or buckets of warm water), and soft sponges and get to it! (Cleaning will never be more fun—promise!)

QUIRKY ACTIVITY

Have class: You may be sick and tired of your own homework, but your local community college most likely offers cool classes, like cooking, sports, photography, and art during the evenings. So look online at the course catalogue for the closest community college, YMCA, or local recreation center, and pick out an evening class you'd both enjoy. You'll bond over doing something fun and new together, and you'll be able to help each other with homework that will actually be fun!

EATING ACTIVITY

Make like Ben & Jerry: You don't have to be a great cook to make great ice cream! All you need is an ice cream maker and basic ingredients like sugar and milk. Check out your local ice cream shop for inspiration, and get started mixing and matching your favorite flavors. Pizza-chocolate-mint, anyone?

Weekend Afternoon Dates

Day-dates offer the most opportunities—you have more time than at night, and you can be outside, too! The secret to great day dates is to take advantage of both of those things. Think of activities you can only do outside, or things you need more than an hour to do.

FREEBIE ACTIVITY

Swing: Head to the nearest playground to push each other on the swings, ride the seesaw, and play in the sandbox. Then, dare him to a game of tetherball—and whoop his butt!

OUTDOORSY ACTIVITY

Root for the home team: Even if you don't live near a major league stadium, chances are there are local sports events to check out in your town—from baseball to hockey to soccer.

Giddyap: Owning a horse may be expensive, but going horseback riding for an afternoon won't cost you more than a night's baby-sitting money. So use the Internet or phone book to find the closest stables—ask them if they have helmets, or if you need to bring your own—then spend the day learning to gallop and trot.

QUIRKY ACTIVITY

Get some culture: You may think that only big cities have museums, but even the smallest towns have exhibits and history museums— sometimes right inside the local library or at the public courthouse. And at a lot of museums, students get free admission. So go online and Google "museum and your city name," call your local library to see if they have or know of current local exhibits, or look in the Yellow Pages under "museum" to see what comes up.

EATING ACTIVITY

Get pickin': Call the nearest orchard or farm to see what fruits or vegetables they have available for picking. In the fall, look for apples and pumpkins. In the summer, look for berries and tomatoes. Certain climates will have great orange, grapefruit, cherry, and peach picking, too. You'll have fun seeking out the best fruit and climbing through leafy patches and up inside trees. And if you're feeling ambitious, you can use your hard-earned fruits to bake a pie together!

Weekend Evening Dates

Movies and dinner aren't the only evening dates out there—you can do *tons* of quirky stuff, like holding movie marathons or cook-offs or game contests. So even if you're not old enough to drive or don't want your parents to drive you anywhere, you can meet at one of your houses and still do more than just stare at the TV!

FREEBIE ACTIVITY

Be a kid again: A few years ago, you were probably always trying to act older. Now that you are a little older, it could be fun to give your old childhood games another shot together. So bust out games like Connect Four, Monopoly, or Sorry. Or tap into your creativity with some finger paints!

OUTDOORSY ACTIVITY

Night-skate: Call your local outdoor ice-skating rink to find out what time they hold public night skating. Then bring your gloves and Thermoses of hot chocolate and skate beneath the stars!

Go to the moon: Or, at least, look at it. Ask your science teacher where you can rent a telescope for the weekend. Then, set up an outdoor nighttime picnic, prop up the telescope, and prepare to see constellations and shooting stars!

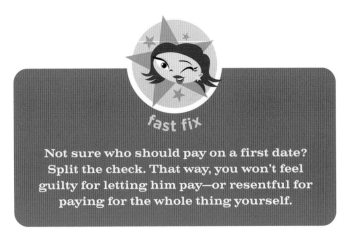

fast fix

Not sure who should pay on a first date?
Split the check. That way, you won't feel
guilty for letting him pay—or resentful for
paying for the whole thing yourself.

QUIRKY ACTIVITY

Hold a screening:
Head to the local video store (or your library's DVD section) and take out Oscar award-winning movies from the years each of you were born. Then, dig into a huge bowl of popcorn, and dim the lights!

EATING ACTIVITY

Cook-off: Prepare your favorite recipe for each other—whether that means chicken or chocolate-chip cookies—then meet up with your dishes and dig in for a picnic (outside, or even inside!).

A FINAL NOTE

It's easy to get stuck in the same patterns, weekend after weekend and month after month, and forget how much stuff there is to do out there. So keep this in mind:

> Just a little bit of effort can lead to a *lot* more fun
> for you and for him. And while it's always great
> to know you can sit around and do nothing
> with someone and still feel comfortable, doing
> interesting things will add another dimension
> to your relationship—and open your eyes
> to new opportunities and ideas.

getting

friend-ly

When you're in a relationship that makes you feel good, your closest friends will–most of the time–be happy for you and root for you two to stay together. But, sometimes, the hardest part about a new relationship is figuring out how to balance it with your friendships.

Sure, your closest friends just want to see you happy—but they also want to *see* you, and don't want you to disappear and start spending every free minute with Mr. Cutie-pie. And no matter how much they like your new boyfriend, that doesn't mean they'll *always* want to hang out with him—girl talk is *never* the same with a guy around.

You owe it to your friends—and to yourself—to make sure you find a comfortable balance between being a good girlfriend . . . and being a good friend to your girls.

Are You Being a Good Friend?

Take this quiz to find out how well you balance your new boyfriend with your old friends!

---

1. You and your girlfriends have had a movie-night-Friday planned all week. When your boyfriend calls to see if you can hang out that night, you:

   a. Tell him you're hanging out with the girls but would love to see him another night.

   b. Ask him if his guy friends are around, then call your girls to see if they want to all hang out, as a big group.

   c. Cancel on your friends to spend alone-time with your boyfriend.

---

2. The last time you called your best friend was to:

   a. Catch up on everything.

   b. Make plans.

   c. See if she had the homework assignment you forgot to jot down.

---

3. When your best friend calls you crying over a breakup, you:

   a. Tell her you'll be right over to comfort her.

   b. Let her cry her heart out, then reassure her it will all work out.

   c. Start freaking out that this could happen to *you*!

4. If you got three tickets to a concert, you'd give two of them to:

a. Your two best girlfriends.

b. Your boyfriend and your best friend.

c. Your boyfriend and his best friend.

5. The first person you'd call with good news is:

a. Your best friend.

b. Your best friend and boyfriend, on 3-way.

c. Your boyfriend.

SCORING

Tally up your answers. If you picked . . .

Mostly a's: You'd never put a guy before your girls, and your friends love you for that. Just remember that it's okay to stray a little bit from your comfort zone to get to know a guy.

Mostly b's: You're a balancing wizard—you can successfully juggle having a boyfriend and being a good friend. Just remember that it's okay to put *your* interests first sometimes—and that you don't always have to please everyone else around you.

Mostly c's: It's great that you're so into your boyfriend and feel so comfortable sharing good news and cool events with him, but don't forget about the people who were there for you long *before* he came along. Make time to call and hang out with your girls, and make sure you listen to what's going on in *their* lives.

The BF/BFF Balance

Learning to mix your old friends with your new boyfriend can feel overwhelming at first—but with time and some growing pains, you can find a way to balance both. Here's how.

LISTEN UP. It's easy to become unintentionally self-centered when you're in a new relationship. You're excited, and when you're not with your crush, you'll just want to talk about him! But remember that even the *most* supportive friends have their own lives and interests and crushes—don't forget to ask about them, and to be a good listener and cheerleader for your friends. And when you *do* talk about yourself, remember to talk about things *besides* your boyfriend.

MIX THINGS UP. At the start of your relationship, you might want to keep your new boyfriend all to yourself for a million different reasons—because you don't want your friends to flirt with him, because you don't want your friends to judge him, because you don't want him to judge your friends. But once you are officially boyfriend and girlfriend, it's time to see what happens when you give everyone the chance to hang out together. It could be great—your friends could see why you're so gaga for your boyfriend, and your boyfriend can get to see a side of you that only your friends bring out. Or if it doesn't go well—if it's uncomfortable or awkward—at least you'll know that you've made the effort to bring them together.

RESPECT GUY TIME—AND ASK HIM TO RESPECT GIRL TIME. It'll be awesome if you get along with his friends and he gets along with yours. But don't forget how much fun it is to hang out with *just* your girlfriends—and how much his guy friends probably enjoy hanging out as just the guys. If you make sure to have time apart, you won't miss out on valuable friend-time—and he won't feel like he's missing out on time with the boys. Added bonus: Choosing your friends sometimes will show him that you're independent, and encouraging him to have guy-time will show his friends that you're not the kind of girl they should give a hard time!

fast fix

If you feel like, now that you have a boyfriend, your friends are getting closer and leaving *you* out of things, talk to them about it. You won't want to make them feel guilty or awkward, so casually say, "I miss you guys—can we plan a bonding session as soon as humanly possible, to catch up on stuff?"

SHOW AND TELL—SOMETIMES. Being a good friend doesn't mean never talking about your boyfriend to your friends. In fact, it will make your friends feel like they are an important part of your life if you share stuff about your relationship with them. So tell them if you had a great date, or if something hilarious happened, or if he reminds you of one of your friends because of his sense of humor or amazing athletic skills. But unless he has a secret that could cause you or someone else harm, *keep your boyfriend's secrets private*—and remember that, sometimes, keeping details between just the two of you can keep you from letting other people's opinions influence your decisions.

SHOW HER YOU CARE. Think about it: When you have a new guy in your life, you probably go out of your way to do all kinds of cute things for him, right? Well, why not use some of that creative energy to do something cute, every now and then, for your girl friends? Stuff like . . .

Make a photo calendar: Round up your twelve favorite photos of you and your best friend. Then, either bring them to a copy shop, where you can pay to have a photo calendar compiled, or use your own computer scanner and calendar program to make your best friend a personalized calendar that shows her you think of her every day of the year!

Buy her flowers: Flowers don't have to be from a guy to be special. So pick out a simple bouquet—or even just one amazing flower—and surprise your friend with it.

Get pampered: Even if you're not the kind of girl who usually pays much attention to her nails, pick an afternoon to get manicures or pedicures together. You'll have fun catching up, and you'll be forced to sit still, unwind, and relax.

Play DJ: Sit down with your iTunes, and put together a playlist you know she'll love. Then, burn it for her, give it to her, and make a date to rock out in her room, screaming the lyrics, and making up your own crazy words to the melodies!

Sweeten her day: Guys aren't the only ones who deserve Valentine's candy and "just because" cupcakes. So the next time you feel like getting creative in the kitchen, whip up a batch of cupcakes with her initials on them, or a cookie-cake with inside-jokes frosted across the top of it!

A FINAL NOTE

It can be fun to get swept up in the newness and excitement of having a boyfriend. But a good friendship can be the most important relationship of all—and deserves to be nurtured and cherished no matter *what* guy comes along.

So work hard to hold on to your friendships, and do everything in your power to not let guy-drama come between you and your girls. Take time to call and hang out with your friends just like you did *before* you had a boyfriend.

smooch

ing

Kissing is one of the most fun parts of a relationship—but it can also be one of the most stressful.

You worry about whether he's gonna kiss you or if you should kiss him, whether your breath will smell, and if you'll even be any good at it once you do kiss!

Here's how to take the kinks out of kissing and put the smile back in smooching!

What's Your Kissing IQ?

How much do you *really* know about kissing?

Write "T" for true or "F" for false after each question.
Check your answers below!

		TRUE or FALSE?
1.	An "Eskimo Kiss" refers to two people rubbing their elbows together.	
2.	The tongue is a muscle.	
3.	A "Butterfly Kiss" refers to people rubbing noses together.	
4.	A Japanese company invented an electronic bad breath detector.	
5.	The record for the longest kiss according to *The Guinness Book of World Records* is more than thirty hours!	
6.	Mono (mononucleosis) is spread through saliva.	
7.	The phrase "French Kiss" dates back to 500 BC.	

S. W. A. K.

Answers:
1. F
2. T
3. F
4. T
5. T
6. T
7. F

Making a Fresh Start

It takes two people to kiss—which means you can't put all the pressure on yourself to create magic. But you'll feel more sure of your half of the deal if you take control of the one factor you actually can change—your breath.

So . . . if you know you'll be in a situation where a kissing opportunity may crop up, make sure to have at least one of the following on hand.

GUM: Fruity gums may taste the best, but minty, sugar-free gums will keep your breath freshest.

MINTS: Look for sugar-free mints that will dissolve in your mouth, that you won't have to crunch down on.

BREATHSTRIPS: Breathstrips are strong, concentrated doses of mouthwash. They come in all kinds of fresh flavors, from mint to cinnamon, and they're tiny enough to slip into your back pocket or even into your sock.

SPRAYS: Sprays last long, and won't overpower your mouth with too much taste.

And remember that as boring as it may be, you should floss, brush, and rinse with mouthwash at least every morning and every night!

PS: In case you needed another reason not to take up a gross habit like smoking, you should know that no guy wants to kiss a smoker—it tastes like licking an ashtray. Nasty!!!

How to Give Great Kisses

There's no right or wrong way to kiss, but these tips will keep you calm—and your kissing sessions fun!

KEEP IT SIMPLE. Kissing shouldn't feel like an athletic event! There are no tricks you need to do with your tongue or "moves" you need to perfect with your lips. Just go with the flow, and let the chemistry between you and your crush do the work.

MIX THINGS UP. You don't need to give your tongue a workout (see above), and a good kiss doesn't have to involve tongue-action at all. Which is why you shouldn't be afraid to include more than one kind of kiss in your makeout sessions. If you're kissing each other's lips, why not stop and kiss his ear, or his cheek, or even his eye (if it's closed!)?

BE PIONEERS. If you're a pro at the basics already, why not challenge your crush to invent a new kiss? First, he has to invent one and try it on you; then, you show him a new one.

PLAY GAMES. Dare your crush to kiss you for a full minute, or to kiss with your eyes open, or to kiss with one eye open and the other one closed.

PRACTICE, PRACTICE, PRACTICE. When you're first starting out kissing, things may go wrong—but everyone gets better over time, so don't think that one bad kiss means you're doomed forever.

Worried that, now that you're open to kissing, the physical stuff might move too fast for you? Then be honest with him. Tell him that it's really fun to be snugly and cuddly with him, but that you're just not ready for much more than kissing. If you bring the topic up on your own terms and nip it in the bud, you won't have to be nervous each time the physical stuff starts—instead, you'll be able to enjoy it with the comfort and knowledge that he knows your boundaries.

A FINAL NOTE

When it comes to magical makeout sessions and sensational smooching, keep this tip in your back pocket:

The most important thing to remember
when it comes to kissing is to *not* overthink it.
Every kiss you have will be different—
and will teach you something to do or not to
do the next time!

giving

great gifts

The best part of your birthday and the holidays is probably getting gifts—but, sometimes, the hardest part of a relationship (especially a new one) is figuring out what kind of gift to get a guy.

On the one hand, you want him to know you think he's terrific. On the other hand, you don't want to freak him out with something too personal, fancy, or expensive. Finding just the right present is not always easy. So here are some tips to help you give the greatest gifts ever!

What's the Best Gift for Him?

To get the guy in your life a present he'll love, start by taking this quiz.

1. His dream car is most likely:
   a. A VW Bug.
   b. Vintage.
   c. A Jeep.

2. Which shoes best match his personality?
   a. Flip flops.
   b. Converse.
   c. Running sneakers.

3. He unwinds by:
   a. Talking.
   b. Reading.
   c. Biking.

4. What's his favorite channel?
   a. Comedy Central.
   b. Independent Film Channel.
   c. ESPN.

5. He'd love to spend spring break:	
a. Throwing a party.	
b. Traveling.	
c. Hiking.	
6. You can always count on him to:	
a. Crack you up.	
b. Teach you something.	
c. Get your butt off the couch.	

SCORING

If you picked . . .

Mostly a's:

MR. OUTGOING loves having fun, talking to people, and putting other people at ease. If you've been dating for less than a month, get him a funny toy that he'll get a kick out of, like Silly Putty or a water gun. If you've been together longer, consider getting him his favorite funny DVD, or even a portable Ping-Pong set.

Mostly b's:

MR. CURIOUS is one-of-a-kind and loves learning new things. If you've been together less than a month, get him a disposable camera and mini-photo album. If you've been together for a while, consider buying him a used or inexpensive new record player, so that he can start exploring original vinyl records, or a special book of photos, poems, or short stories.

Mostly c's:

MR. ATHLETIC is always keeping busy. If you've been together for less than a month, get him a bobblehead of his favorite athlete; he'll appreciate that you've been paying attention to his passions. Together longer? Track down an authentic jersey, or tickets to an upcoming sporting event for the two of you.

Picking the Perfect Present

When it comes to buying a guy a gift, there are really only three questions you have to answer.

1. **What is he into?** Think about his personality, his interests, his goals, and his hobbies.

2. **How long have you been dating?** If you're buying a gift for a relatively new boyfriend, you'll want to get him something that he'll like—and that shows you're interested in getting to know him better. You don't want to go overboard, or scare him away. But if you've been dating longer—like, more than six months— you'll want to put extra thought into your gift, and get him something that shows him how well you really know him and that you're willing to go out of your way for him.

3. **How much should you spend?** This is a question of both money, and time. For a new guy, you probably shouldn't have to break more than a twenty-dollar bill, or spend more than an afternoon shopping or making something. For someone you've been with longer, you may feel comfortable putting aside a bit more cash, or devoting extra time to making something sentimental and one-of-a-kind.

That's a Wrap!

You can't judge a book by its cover, but you *can* spice up even the simplest gifts with creative wrapping. So for a guy you've been seeing for a while, try one of these ideas to jazz up the next present you give him.

PUT THE GIFT INSIDE HIS FAVORITE CEREAL OR COOKIE BOX. Is he a Cheerios fan? Buy a box, take out the cereal from inside, and wrap your present inside.

USE HIS FAVORITE MAGAZINE/NEWSPAPER FOR WRAPPING PAPER. Does he read the sports section every Monday, or read *Rolling Stone* obsessively? Buy the latest issue, and use a few pages as wrapping paper.

INDULGE HIS SWEET TOOTH. If your crush is a candy **junkie,** treat his gift like a gingerbread house, and cover it with wrapped candies he'll love. First, wrap the gift in plain paper—construction paper or even freezer-wrap will do. Then, take his favorite wrapped candies and use double-sided tape to stick them to the wrapping (you can spell something out with the candies, or just put them on randomly). And remember: Don't use any kind of candy that's not in a wrapper or will melt. *Ewww!*

TAKE A WALK DOWN MEMORY LANE. If you've been together for a while, cover the gift with plain white paper, then tape to it mementos from your time together—like ticket stubs from movies you've been to, or inside jokes only he'll get!

COLLAGE. Cut out pictures and words he'll appreciate from old magazines and newspapers, then tape or glue them to plain paper and wrap your gift with it.

Dealing with a Dud Gift

Everyone faces at least *one* holiday or birthday when their crush gives them a clunker gift—the kind that makes you wonder how well he really knows you . . . and how well you really know him! But if you're confident that his intentions are good (and that his taste in "stuff" just might be bad), keep these tips in mind.

SAY SOMETHING POSITIVE—AND HONEST—ABOUT WHAT HE GAVE YOU. If you hate the pink sparkly belt he gave you but love the color pink, say, "Aw, pink is my favorite color." Or if he buys you a CD you hate or already have, don't tell him that—just say, "You know how obsessed I am with building up my music stash." Focus on saying something that's truthful, *and* won't hurt his feelings.

fast fix

If your guy gets you a gift for an occasion and you didn't even think to get *him* anything, don't panic. Instead, thank him for being so thoughtful. Later that day, send him a small thank-you present. You'll want to show him that you're being appreciative— not that you two have to go tit-for-tat for everything!

DON'T RETURN IT—UNLESS HE'LL ABSOLUTELY NEVER FIND OUT. Unless he got you something you already have, don't bother trying to get store credit or money for his gift. Even if you don't use it, think of it as a sentimental memento.

USE IT OR WEAR IT IN FRONT OF HIM—ONCE. You don't have to start wearing a perfume that smells like wet-dog every day just because he got it for you. But do make a point of using or wearing his gift at least *once* in front of him. It will send the message that you're appreciative of his efforts to go out of his way for you. You don't want to discourage him from buying presents in the future—or make him doubt his ability to give gifts. If you reward his efforts to go out of his way for you, chances are he'll do it again . . . and practice makes perfect, right?

NEXT TIME, DROP HINTS—AND DON'T EXPECT HIM TO READ YOUR MIND. Every girl wants to believe that her boyfriend knows her so well and has such great taste that *of course* he'll pick out a perfect gift without needing any help or suggestions. But when it comes to picking out gifts, the sad truth is that *most* guys are, well, bad at it. If your guy falls into this majority, don't be afraid to guide him to what you want next time. Don't flat out say, "I want this hat for Christmas," or, "I'd love this shirt for my birthday." But do make comments like, "I love the color green!" or, "I have to remember to ask Santa for new stationery."

A FINAL NOTE

As corny as the expression, "It's the thought that counts," may be, there really is truth to it. So remember:

The effort you and he put into your gifts
says *way* more than the gift itself (or the price
tag of it!) ever could.

saying

buh-bye

The worst part of any relationship is the end of it. Whether you're the one ending it or a guy ends it with you, breakups come with a natural mix of sadness, guilt, insecurity, doubt, and awkwardness.

And while all of that sounds pretty miserable, there *is* some good that comes out of breakups. Because once you get past the shock or the tears or the jealousy, what you will eventually realize is that every relationship teaches you something. Breakups force everyone to reflect on the past, and in thinking about the past, you'll be able to learn for the future. Some breakups will teach you what you want and don't want; some will help you learn something about yourself; some will show you who your true friends are. And all breakups will make you realize that you can get through even the hardest times with patience, good friends, and welcome distractions.

Is It Time to Break Up?

Do you get excited when you see his name on your caller ID?

TOTALLY! → Does he give you the attention you want?

UM, NAH . . . → Are you jealous of the "freedom" your single friends have?

NOT REALLY / NOPE → Do you secretly have a crush on another guy?

YOU BET!

YUP!

NOT UNLESS YOU COUNT ORLANDO BLOOM!

YES—SHH! → Do you make excuses not to hang out with him?

Do you know him better now than when you first got together?

Do you have to remind yourself why you like him?

NO

YES

NOT SO MUCH

YES

NO

YES

SMOOTH SAILING You are still so into him that it wouldn't even occur to you to break up with him! Keep enjoying your relationship, and save this chapter for another day!

ROCKY ROAD You're definitely not as into him as you once were or would like to be. If you want to make things work out, talk about it with him. But if your feelings don't change over the next few weeks, you may want to ask yourself why you are with him.

Making the Best of a Breakup

There's no doubt that breakups are painful, but the following tips can help you get through them.

If You're the One Doing the Breaking Up:

DO IT IN PERSON. Sure, it would be a lot less painful to deal with *every* sticky situation through skywriting or passing notes. But you owe it to someone who's a part of your life to break up in person.

DON'T DRAG YOUR FEET. Once you've decided in your heart that it's time to break up, don't put it off or create excuses or start treating him badly in the hopes that you can trick *him* into breaking up with *you* instead.

DON'T TURN THINGS AROUND. If you're breaking up with him because he didn't treat you right, feel free to tell him that. But if you're breaking up with him because of reasons that aren't his fault—because you like someone else, or because you want to be free to see other guys—don't invent a problem or blame him for something he didn't do.

(continued on the next page)

BE HONEST. Be as open as possible—without going out of your way to tell him things that might hurt his feelings even more—when you break up with him. Tell him something specific and honest and positive about your relationship, like, "You have the best sense of humor and always know how to make me laugh." Then, segue into the bad news, "But, lately, I just don't think it's the right time for me to be in a relationship," or "But I've decided that I felt more comfortable when we were just friends."

DON'T SPILL EVERYTHING. You may feel so guilty that you'll want to tell him every last thing that led to your decision to end your relationship. But remember that you can break up without totally traumatizing him. Stay away from rattling off every annoying flaw you discovered or all the things you like better about *other* guys!

DON'T MAKE EMPTY PROMISES. You may feel like you have to keep talking or give some kind of hope for the future—but if you know you really don't want to get back together, don't even hint at the possibility. Even if you think it will make him less mad at you, remember that it's not fair to have everything your way—you're entitled to break up with him, but he's entitled to be angry or upset with you for doing so. Don't expect to break up with him *and* have him still think you're perfect in every way.

If Someone's Just Broken Up with *You:*

DO ASK FOR AN EXPLANATION—BUT DON'T EXPECT TO GET ONE. If your boyfriend confronts you with his decision to break up and it seems to come out of nowhere, don't be shy about asking for an explanation. But be realistic: Chances are, he might not want to tell you the exact reasons for his feelings—and he may not fully understand them himself!

DO SHARE YOUR HONEST REACTION. If you're hurt, tell him. Surprised? Express that. Angry? You have a right to be. Your feelings are normal and natural, and you don't have to pretend to be okay with the news or try to console *him* about a decision that upsets you. Remember: *Your* feelings should come first in this situation, not his.

DON'T SEEK REVENGE. You know that expression, "Do unto others as you'd want them to do unto you"? Well, no matter how angry a breakup gets you, keep that rule in mind. Because there's nothing good that can come from getting even. The best thing to do is focus on doing things to make you feel better.

LET YOURSELF BE SAD. It's unrealistic to expect to feel great immediately after a breakup. You need time to process what happened, and to think about how it will change things in the future. So don't rush to immediately be "fine"—let yourself listen to sad music, cry to your friends, and write in your journal. Then, after two weeks of indulging your sadness, promise yourself that you'll do whatever it takes to stop letting yourself feel bad all of the time— and that you'll focus every day on doing at least one fun, new, different, or indulgent thing. That's not to say you won't feel sad after two weeks—but you should start focusing on being happy.

DON'T HANG OUT WITH HIM. Those just might be the hardest five words in this whole book to listen to. But force yourself not to call him, e-mail him, or hang out with him. It will only keep you from moving on and make you feel insecure and angry—just seeing him will be a reminder of all the ways the breakup made you feel rotten. So unless you *have* to be around him for school or work stuff, *avoid him*. It may seem like if you hang out, he'll remember why he needs you as his girlfriend. And that *may* be true. But do you really want to be with someone who hurt you and needs to be *convinced* that you're great? No!

DON'T TRY TO BE FRIENDS WITH HIS NEW GIRLFRIEND. You may think this will give you a connection to your ex and prove that you're cool with things . . . but, c'mon. You have a ton of great girlfriends already and trying to be her friend will just mean that you'll have to see and hear about him—and didn't we just talk about why you *shouldn't* be around him anymore?

Pamper Yourself

After a breakup, you should go out of your way to do things that make you feel good about yourself. Try some of these post-breakup pick-me-ups:

BRIGHTEN THINGS UP. Ask a parent if you can paint one or all of the walls in your bedroom a bright, airy color—like yellow or lime green. If not, head to the closest art supply store, and buy a few pieces of posterboard in a bright color. Then, use tape to stick the boards to your closet doors, ceiling, or around your room—just looking at vibrant colors will cheer you up, and the change in scenery will help you feel like you're making a fresh start.

DANCE. Even if you have two left feet, dancing in the privacy of your own room for five minutes every day will instantly make you feel better—the physical workout will release endorphins, or "feel-good hormones," into your system, and singing and dancing along to your favorite upbeat songs will give you the chance to release pent-up frustration and stress.

MAKE A FRESH-FRUIT SMOOTHIE. Eating junk food when you're feeling down may seem comforting—but after a while, it will only make you feel tired and sluggish. Instead, ask a parent if you can use the blender to whip up a fruit smoothie—mix your favorite fruits with either ice or frozen yogurt or a combo of both—then give your new concoction a funny name, and enjoy!

GET SOME FRESH AIR. Even if it's the dead of winter and it's freezing cold outside, taking a deep breath of fresh air can refresh *and* relax you. So make time for outdoor walks, or simply open the front door, close your eyes, inhale deeply, and then let the sadness out of your body as you exhale.

GIVE YOGA A TRY. Yoga may seem boring or slow, or like it will make you feel restless and impatient. But if you approach it with an open mind, it can teach you how to stay calm and focused on what's good in your life and the world around you. So sign up for a beginner's class at your local YMCA or rec center, or borrow a yoga DVD from your local library.

A FINAL NOTE

Give yourself time to get over the end of a relationship. And remember this:

Instead of rushing to find a new guy (or begging the old guy to make it work), use breakup time to focus on *you*, your friends, and all the things you loved to do even before Mr. You-Know-Who entered the picture.

trouble

shooting

When it comes to guys and relationships, you're always going to hit some bumpy patches.

We could all use a relationship road map sometimes, with directions for navigating everything from cheating boyfriends to getting back together with an ex to making a long-distance relationship work. There are so many twists and turns. So buckle up, and let's hit the rocky road!

problem: A guy friend tells you he likes you more than a friend—but you don't feel the same way about him.

solution: Be honest. Don't make up an excuse or give him false hope. It's flattering when a guy-friend showers you with attention, but it's selfish to make him think he has a chance just because you like the ego boost he gives you.

So say, "I'm so flattered that you see me that way, and that you feel comfortable telling me. It makes me feel like our friendship is really special. That's why I need to be 100 percent honest with you and tell you that as funny/smart/adorable as I think you are, I just don't have romantic feelings about us. I don't mean that harshly, and I hope my saying that doesn't make you mad. I'll understand if you want some time away from me, but I hope we can get over any weirdness and be our normal selves again soon—because I'd miss you too much if we didn't continue to hang out."

problem: You confess to a guy that you like him—but he doesn't feel the same way.

solution: You may feel embarrassed, disappointed, or, well, insulted. And the only way to counter those feelings is to take control of undoing them. So . . . to combat your embarrassment and disappointment, ask your crush to keep your conversation between the two of you. (Say, "I know we can't pretend that conversation never happened, but can you not tell anyone *else* about it?") Then do something that always cheers you up. Read a magazine, or watch your favorite DVD for the eight billionth time.

As for feeling insulted, do something *rewarding*. Offer to teach your sister a new dance; bead a necklace for your mom; or call your grandma just to say hi. The feeling—and gratitude—you'll get when you do things for others will remind you that there are tons of people who *do* appreciate you.

problem: You want to figure out how to make a long-distance relationship—or a relationship with someone at another school—work, without always stressing about it.

solution: Before you decide to be in a long-distance relationship, ask yourself if you'd be happy in a relationship with someone you don't get to see every day in school—or if you'd rather hold out for someone you'd get to see more often. And decide if you trust your crush enough not to always wonder if he's flirting with other girls. Then ask yourself if you really care about the relationship—or if you're just holding on to it because you'd rather have a long-distance boyfriend than no boyfriend.

If you answer these questions and still want to give long-distance a try, keep these tips in mind: First, go out of your way to do nice things for each other—surprise each other with small, cute gifts and cards. Second, when you make plans to see each other, build in enough time to do fun stuff—but also to just hang out and talk. Third, introduce him to your friends and family—that way, you won't start to feel like he's a separate part of your life. And, lastly, don't put too much pressure on yourself—or him. You'll want each time you see each other to be amazing. But life's not perfect—everyone wakes up feeling stressed, or moody, or with a big zit on their nose, even on special days that are supposed to be flawless.

problem: Your ex is hanging out with someone new—and your jealousy has reached levels you never imagined possible!

solution: Jealousy can consume even the most confident and otherwise levelheaded girls—but it's the kind of irrational and useless emotion that usually leads to nothing positive or productive. The only cure for jealousy is time—you *will* grow out of it—but the best fix in the meantime is distraction. So as soon as the jealousy bug hits you, throw yourself into something else. Hang out with friends, paint your room, experiment with a new recipe . . . *anything* that will keep your mind from wandering. And since a jealousy funk can have a way of taking a toll on your self-esteem, go out of your way to spend time with people who make you feel great—your parents, your girlfriends, your siblings, even your adorable puppy! Because when you're in jealous mode, you need and deserve all the extra hugs and love you can get!

problem: You cheat on your boyfriend—and it's made you realize you want to break up with him.

solution: First, face up to the truth: if you cheated on your boyfriend, there's a *reason* you did it. Maybe you long for newness and excitement, maybe you don't feel ready to be with just one person, maybe the guy you cheated with has some trait that's important to you but missing in your boyfriend. Even if you regret your slip-up, it most likely points to the fact that you're really *not* ready to be in an exclusive relationship with your boyfriend.

So it's time to break the bad news. Ask your boyfriend to go for a walk. Then, tell him there's something you need to talk about, and without building up any more suspense, say, "I cheated on you." Don't feel like you have to tell him intimate details or answer questions he may *think* he wants the answer to. Just explain that you know you made a mistake, but that it's made you realize you're really not ready to be in a relationship—and that it wouldn't be fair to him if you continued to be together. Expect your boyfriend to be *very* angry and upset. But don't feel like you deserve to be treated badly—just focus on doing the right thing to make up for doing the wrong thing. And the right thing is giving *both* of you time and space apart from each other.

problem: You cheat on your boyfriend—but want to convince him to stay together.

solution: If you cheated but really want to stay together despite your mistake, you'll have to work hard to regain his trust. So, tell him what you did; apologize and explain that it had *nothing* to do with him, and that you wish you could take it back, but since you can't, you want to focus on earning back his trust. Know that your boyfriend might be so wounded that he'll refuse to give it a try. But offer to give him time to think about your apology and your commitment to proving that things can work. Then, make sure you never cheat on your boyfriend again. He may take you back once, but it's not something *anyone* would want to make a habit of.

problem: You find out your boyfriend cheated on you.

solution: The bizarre part of being cheated on is that it *should* make you want nothing to do with the guy—but, sometimes, especially if your boyfriend has always been loyal and amazing in the past, it leaves you so stunned, confused, and jealous that you start latching on even tighter. But giving a cheater a second chance right away can be a recipe for disaster.

So . . . hard as it may be, the best thing to do if you've been two-timed is to take a break from your boyfriend at least for now. Then, give him time to *prove* that he deserves a second chance. If he continues to pursue you and be patient with you and doesn't just move on to a new girl right away, you'll know that he's worth giving just one more chance. But if you see for yourself that he's out flirting with every other girl out there, at least you'll have spared yourself the drama of making the same mistake twice.

problem: You want to get back together with an ex!

solution: It's normal to have lingering or reignited feelings for an ex. Even if things ended badly, time and distance can make you see only his redeeming qualities and remember the good stuff as being even better than it was. But before you rush to get back together with an ex, ask yourself this: Did things fall apart the last time because he made you feel bad about yourself, or unfairly hurt your feelings? If so, did you ever talk about it with him? If you didn't, it's time to bring up the stuff that may hurt or be awkward, so that you can get answers—and, possibly, an apology. Afterall, people can deserve second chances—if they prove that they understand their mistakes and want to try to avoid them in the future. If things didn't end badly—if they just ended because you grew apart, or because you wanted to see other people, or because there just wasn't that much of a spark—then it's time to get to know each other again. So don't rush into making out or back to the familiar parts of your old relationship—spend time getting to know each other's *new* interests and friends, to see if you really do have a connection that makes it worth giving a relationship another try.

problem: You think you might have a crush on one of your boyfriend's friends.

solution: At some point, almost every girl develops a crush on one of her boyfriend's friends. (No one likes to admit it, but it's just one of those universal truths!) It's a sticky situation, but it also makes perfect sense that your boyfriend would have good taste in friends (if he's dating you, he obviously has good taste, right?). The only way to deal with this scenario is to ask yourself the following: *Do you like your boyfriend's friend more than you like your boyfriend?* If not, force yourself to stop flirting with his friend. You don't have to go out of your way to avoid him, but don't be physical or go *out* of your way to forge a separate friendship. It will only confuse *everyone*.

If you find yourself realizing that you *do* have stronger feelings for his friend than him, you owe it to yourself and your boyfriend to break up (flip back to the chapter "Saying Buh-Bye"). But don't break up with your boyfriend and then rush into trying to date his friend. *Everyone* needs time alone after a breakup—and rushing into an ex's friend's arms is not only insensitive to your ex, but risky for your mindset (and reputation). So give yourself a month to get over your relationship before you start thinking about—or flirting with—*anyone* new. (The point isn't that you'd be breaking up with your boyfriend to be with his friend; it's that you're breaking up with him because you realize he doesn't hold your interest as much as someone else out there could.)

problem: Your boyfriend wants you to meet his parents, and you're totally nervous about it!

solution: It's a huge compliment when a guy feels comfortable enough to let his parents into his personal life. And if you're really into him, of course it's going to stress you out to try to make a good impression. (Of course, if the reason you're freaked out is because you *don't* feel as strongly about him as he does about you, remember this: Just because you meet his parents, that doesn't mean you're bound to him forever or that you "owe" him your endless devotion!) Whatever you're feeling, stop focusing on the future and instead focus on getting through the present. Because whether you're feeling flattered or freaked out, here's how to survive meeting his parents:

MIND YOUR MANNERS. No matter how casual his parents seem, call them "Mr." and "Mrs." (or "Dr." or "Mr. President" or whatever their titles may be); say "please" and "thank you"; offer to help (set the table, clear the table, refill the water pitcher).

KEEP YOUR HANDS OFF THEIR SON. Use every ounce of willpower in you not to touch, kiss, or hang all over your boyfriend in front of his parents.

SHARE SOMETHING ABOUT YOURSELF. Tell them about a piano recital you have coming up, or how your soccer team is preparing to play its biggest rival next week.

TAKE AN INTEREST IN THEM. Find out beforehand what their interests are—then ask about them, while making eye contact and showing a sincere interest in their answer.

AVOID SENSITIVE SUBJECTS. Money, religion, and politics are never good "meet-the-parents" topics, so don't be the one to bring them up. And ask your boyfriend in advance if there's anything you should know or be aware of before meeting them.

BRING SOMETHING. Whether it's a small bouquet of flowers or cookies from your favorite bakery, bring along a small token of appreciation.

A FINAL NOTE

Every relationship has its share of sticky situations. But you can take comfort in the fact that:

For better or worse, it usually just takes time, patience, and a little bit of humor to get through even the trickiest scenarios.

the final exam

Now that you've mastered the most common sticky situations and have the tools for surviving every guy scenario out there, it's time for a little "final exam"! Think back on the tips, tricks, and "fast fixes" you've picked up, and jot down your answers to this pop quiz.

1. When all else fails or you're stumped for something to say to your crush, you should:
  a. Ignore him.
  b. Pretend to be on your cell phone.
  c. Ask him a question.

2. When meeting your boyfriend's parents for the first time, don't bring up:
  a. Politics.
  b. Religion.
  c. Either of the above.

3. If a guy gets you a gift you hate, you should:
  a. Tell him.
  b. Thank him.
  c. Return it.

4. A great kiss always involves:
  a. Tongues.
  b. Talking.
  c. Confidence.

5. The only way to keep your friends once you get a boyfriend is to:

   a. Tell them everything about your new relationship.

   b. Keep your friends and your boyfriend separate.

   c. Pay attention to what's going on in your friends' lives.

6. The best way to break up with someone is:

   a. Over e-mail.

   b. By telling him exactly why you're over him.

   c. Neither of the above.

7. Long-distance relationships are:

   a. Doomed.

   b. Challenging—but rewarding.

   c. Boring.

2 or less right: Hey, Juliet—you can and will land yourself a Romeo some day, but it looks like you have some homework to do. Start by re-reading the "Fast Fix" and "A Final Note" sections of this book.

3–5 right: You're on the road to being a relationship goddess—time, practice, and experience will have you there in no time!

6–7 right: Hello, lovergirl! You understand that the secret to dealing with guys is patience, respect, and confidence, and you're working to build all three even more. Have fun doing it!

Answers: C, C, B, C, C, B

extra credit!

Now, it's time to party— because you've realized that as stressful as guy stuff can be, the best part of guys and relationships is how much fun they can bring to your life! So on these next few pages, it's time to kick back and relax.

Get the Scoop!

Love and relationships have been around forever—and won't ever disappear! Which means that no matter how different you may feel from your parents or grandparents or younger siblings or cousins or friends, you can *all* relate to the power of love and relationships.

So, on a separate piece of paper, "interview" your girl friends and the women in your family about guys and love and relationships. Ask them who their first crush was, when they had their first kiss, how they would describe falling in love, what their first date was, and what they wish they could do differently or over again when it comes to guys and love. You might pick up a few tricks and, at the very least, you'll learn new things about the people you only *think* you know everything about.

WORD SEARCH

Can you find all of the hidden guy scenarios (look up, down, across, diagonal—and backwards!)?

ASKING HIM OUT, BREAKING UP, CHEATING, CRUSH, E-MAIL, EX-BOYFRIEND, FIRST DATE, FLIRTING, FRESH BREATH, GIFTS, GROUP DATE, HEART, JEALOUSY, KISSING, LOVE, LOVE SONGS, SPLITTING THE BILL, TROUBLESHOOTING, TTYL, XXOO

```
F R S T D T E Y R U O N T P M E E D U N K H E I R
A H L X O X B R E A K I I P L T T I O L P N S O O
G A I E P E E E R H U T U O M I H G N I K S A R L
R R J R S T P I N O N P K I T R X O N E J M U D L
I T Y E X F R E S H B R E A T H T E N T L I G U I
L K U A O R X E E X R O A X X O O I H C A T M W N
L I I K E S X V J K O M M W O W I D T H T O T T G
L Y H I M S B V E X P G J E R S T F I G U O O D R
X E J N A S R E S L E M U J E A L O U S Y O U M O
O L L N I T E R I O L P T S X I X S O W C L Y S U
L A L G L D A Y K V I T O O R R O Y N H A J R S P
M N I U X A A I A E N T A T X U O P T T R A U I D
N N B O X T L N C S N R I X J H A P T S A N N M A
I M E P K A I T H O G N E T O E O Y T N I N K E T
J Y H K I H X S S N G I D M X A L J T E N N L O E
U U T I S U X M N G X I A I O R X O D W Y E E V K
M I G S S L C R U S H P R R T T V G L W F T M Y J
T W N S I K H E A R R T T G I F N I N U A A W O D
A H I S N W E X B O Y F R I E N D F T T R D N T U
Q E T S G E A X H S C W U I N O U F I D G T T O O
I D T S T E T P R O M E G U M X C F R H O S Y U R
D W I S J K I C H E A P T P U G N I K A E R B Y T
F R L I P I N R U S M O O M T E V O L I I I T O T
J Y P U N J G O C E F I R T F L U R T M M F T T H
H H S T Y M G N I T O O H S E L B U O R T I L O F
```

(answers on page 94)

Guilty Pleasures

For all those times you're feeling boy crazy—but don't have a boy to go crazy with or over—here are goofy, guilt-free guy activities to indulge in with your girlfriends or on your own.

1. Make a playlist of the best love songs you can think of, and make a copy for you and all your friends.

2. Go to your library or bookstore and get a book of love poems. Write the most beautiful, inspiring verses you find on a piece of paper and put them above your mirror or inside your notebook, or someplace where you'll see them every day.

3. Learn how to say the word "love" in twenty different languages. Ask your librarian or a bookstore staffer to help you find foreign language dictionaries.

4. Invent a "love potion" smoothie or summer drink with your best friend, using fruits, juices, ice, and other ingredients you have in your fridge. Give it a name that only the two of you get!

5. Head to a crowded public place like a mall or beach with your best friend, and dare each other to talk to five new guys who are your age.

Guy Time Capsule

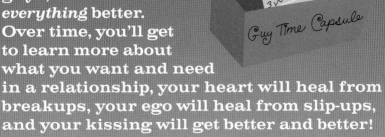

When it comes to guys, time makes *everything* better. Over time, you'll get to learn more about what you want and need in a relationship, your heart will heal from breakups, your ego will heal from slip-ups, and your kissing will get better and better!

And because you—and the guys you like and relationships you want—are going to change tons over the years, take time *now* to make a Teen Girl's Gotta-Have-It Guy Time Capsule.

1. Find an old shoebox.

2. Inside, put a picture of your current crush and pictures from magazines of your celebrity crushes. Write a list of the "Top Five Most Important Traits" you look for in a guy, and a list of questions to ask yourself in ten years, like "What's the most important lesson you've learned about guys in the last ten years?" and "In what way do boys never really change—no matter how old they are?" and "What are the five most important traits you look for in a guy *now*?"

3. Seal the box with heavy-duty tape and write "Private!" on it.

4. Ask a parent to hold it for ten years, or, tuck it away in the bottom of your closet, where you'll forget about it for the next decade!

```
F R S T D T E Y R U O N T P M E E D U N K H E I R
A H L X O X B R E A K I I P L T T I O L P N S O O
G A I E P E E E R H U T U O M I H G N I K S A R L
R R J R S T P I N O N P K I T R X O N E J M U D L
I T Y E X F R E S H B R E A T H T E N T L I G U I
L K U A O R X E E X R O A X X O O I H C A T M W N
L I I K E S X V J K O M M W O W I D T H T O T T G
L Y H I M S B V E X P G J E R S T F I G U O O D R
X E J N A S R E S L E M U J E A L O U S Y O U M O
O L L N I T E R I O L P T S X I X S O W C L Y S U
L A L G L D A Y K V I T O O R R O Y N H A J R S P
M N I U X A A I A E N T A T X U O P T T R A U I D
N N B O X T L N C S N R I X J H A P T S A N N M A
I M E P K A I T H O G N E T O E O Y T N I N K E T
J Y H K I H X S S N G I D M X A L J T E N N L O E
U U T I S U X M N G X I A I O R X O D W Y E E V K
M I G S S L C R U S H P R R T T V G L W F T M Y J
T W N S I K H E A R R T T G I F N I N U A A W O D
A H I S N W E X B O Y F R I E N D F T T R D N T U
Q E T S G E A X H S C W U I N O U F I D G T T O O
I D T S T E T P R O M E G U M X C F R H O S Y U R
D W I S J K I C H E A P T P U G N I K A E R B Y T
F R L I P I N R U S M O O M T E V O L I I I T O T
J Y P U N J G O C E F I R T F L U R T M M F T T H
H H S T Y M G N I T O O H S E L B U O R T I L O F
```

the 411

Looking for more info on guys, dating, love, romance, and advice?

Here are some of our favorite resources. And remember—some of the best resources are right in front of you: Your parents! No matter how awkward you think it may be to talk to them, remember that they were once in your shoes—and that they're there to help, love, and support you. And don't be shy to ask your guidance counselor or school psychologist if you're ever looking for advice or professional help for matters of the heart or matters of any other kind— that's what they're there for.

THE ART OF KISSING
www.kissing.com

PLANNED PARENTHOOD
www.teenwire.com

CHOOSE RESPECT INITIATIVE
www.chooserespect.org

Remember: Call 911 for emergencies or any time you're in immediate danger.

index